M000159863

The Frosty Folks

The Frosty Folks of this charming cross stitch collection would love to bring their playful antics into your home. Want to see how merry your mantel can be? Stitch the jolly **snowman stocking** for each person in your family! You can create a flurry of six **ornaments** for your Christmas tree. Or perhaps you'd prefer to hang a festive **framed piece** in the hall. There are **huck towels** for kitchen or bath, and **bright bibs** for Baby. And you can keep all your precious memories of the season in a **photo album** made cheery with a smiling snow family on the front. Christmas is such a special time of year, and now you can make your holidays "snow" much more fun with cross stitch!

Leisure Arts, Inc.
Little Rock, Arkansas

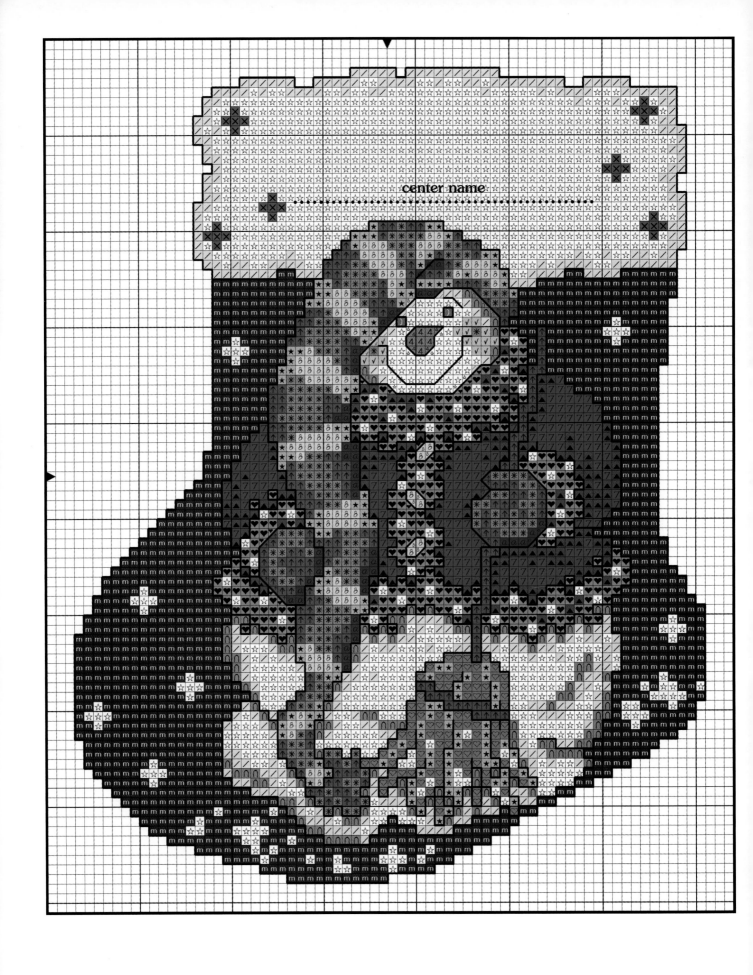

center name

4

Snow Daze

X	DMC	1/4X	B'ST	ANC.	COLOR
☆	blanc	☆		2	white
)	310		/	403	black
↑	321	↑		9046	red
√	353	√		6	pink
♡	680			901	gold
♥	703	♥		238	yellow green
8	726	8		295	yellow
m	796			133	dk blue
X	798			131	blue
a	816	a		1005	maroon
n	932	n		1033	antique blue
4	947	4		330	orange
▲	986	▲		246	dk green
7	987	7		244	green
/	3753	/		1031	baby blue
✱	3801			1098	salmon
★	3821			305	lt gold

Snow Daze was stitched on an 8" x 9¼" piece of 14 count White Aida (design size 5" x 6¼"). Three strands of floss were used for Cross Stitch and one strand for Backstitch. The design was personalized using the alphabet on page 31 and two strands of DMC 310 floss and made into an ornament.

Ornament Finishing Instructions
Trim the stitched piece to desired finished size plus ½" on all sides. Cut fabric for backing the same size. Matching right sides and raw edges and using a ½" seam allowance, sew the stitched piece to backing fabric, leaving an opening for turning. Clip seam allowances. Turn right side out and press. Stuff the ornament with polyester fiberfill and slipstitch the opening closed.

Stitch Count (68w x 85h)

14 count	5"	x	6¼"
16 count	4¼"	x	5½"
18 count	4"	x	4¾"

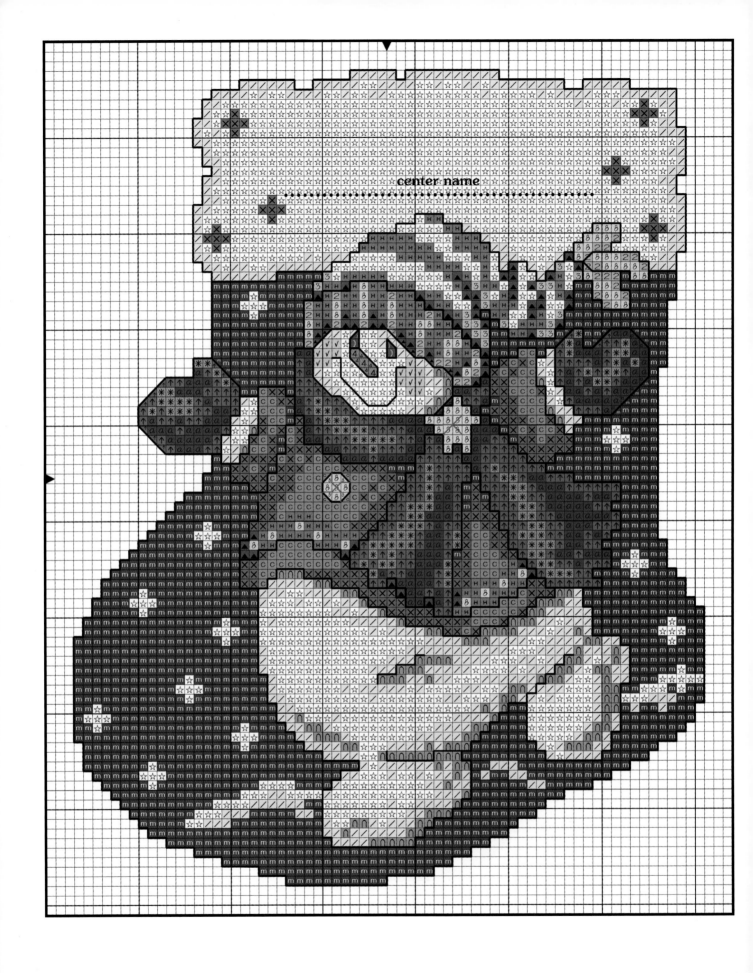

Snow Fun

X	DMC	1/4X	B'ST	ANC.	COLOR
☆	blanc			2	white
)	310		/	403	black
↑	321		/	9046	red
√	353			6	pink
3	415			398	grey
8	726	8		295	yellow
m	796	m		133	dk blue
X	798			131	blue
C	809	c		130	lt blue
a	816			1005	maroon
∩	932	n		1033	antique blue
4	947	4		330	orange
▲	986			246	dk green
H	988			243	green
/	3753			1031	baby blue
✳	3801			1098	salmon
2	3820	2		306	gold

Snow Fun was stitched on an 8" x 9¼" piece of 14 count White Aida (design size 5" x 6¼"). Three strands of floss were used for Cross Stitch and one strand for Backstitch. The design was personalized using the alphabet on page 31 and two strands of DMC 310 floss and made into an ornament.

Ornament Finishing Instructions
Trim the stitched piece to desired finished size plus ½" on all sides. Cut fabric for backing the same size. Matching right sides and raw edges and using a ½" seam allowance, sew the stitched piece to backing fabric, leaving an opening for turning. Clip seam allowances. Turn right side out and press. Stuff the ornament with polyester fiberfill and slipstitch the opening closed.

Stitch Count (68w x 85h)

14 count	5"	x	6¼"
16 count	4¼"	x	5½"
18 count	4"	x	4¾"

center name

Snowball Fight

X	DMC	1/4X	B'ST	ANC.	COLOR
☆	blanc	☆		2	white
)	310		/	403	black
↑	321	◢		9046	red
√	353			6	pink
3	415	3		398	grey
m	796	m		133	dk blue
X	798			131	blue
a	816	◢		1005	maroon
∩	932	∩		1033	antique blue
4	947	◢		330	orange
/	3753	/		1031	baby blue
✳	3801			1098	salmon

Snowball Fight was stitched on an 8" x 9 1/4" piece of 14 count White Aida (design size 5" x 6 1/4"). Three strands of floss were used for Cross Stitch and one strand for Backstitch. The design was personalized using the alphabet on page 31 and two strands of DMC 310 floss and made into an ornament.

Ornament Finishing Instructions

Trim the stitched piece to desired finished size plus 1/2" on all sides. Cut fabric for backing the same size. Matching right sides and raw edges and using a 1/2" seam allowance, sew the stitched piece to backing fabric, leaving an opening for turning. Clip seam allowances. Turn right side out and press. Stuff the ornament with polyester fiberfill and slipstitch the opening closed.

Stitch Count (68w x 85h)

14 count	5"	x 6 1/4"
16 count	4 1/4"	x 5 1/2"
18 count	4"	x 4 3/4"

center name

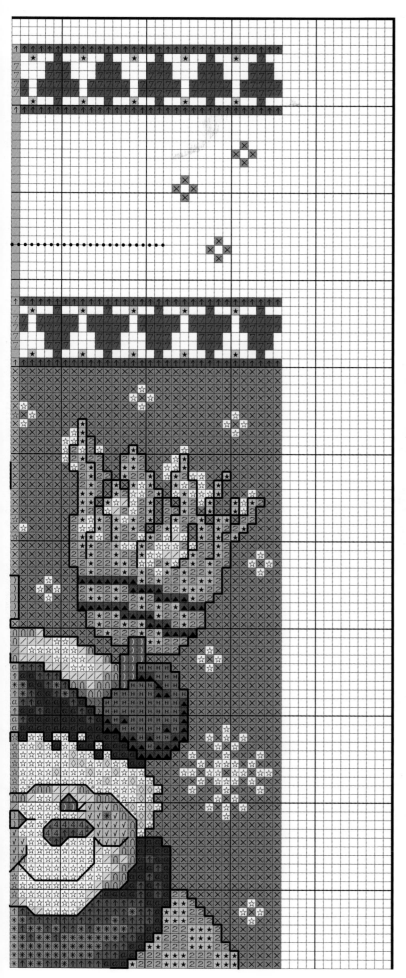

Family Fun

X	DMC	¼X	B'ST	ANC.	COLOR
☆	blanc			2	white
)	310		/	403	black
↑	321			9046	red
√	353	√		6	pink
◇	677			886	tan
♡	680			901	dk gold
8	726			295	yellow
m	796	m		133	dk blue
X	798	X		131	blue
T	800			144	vy lt blue
C	809			130	lt blue
a	816			1005	maroon
>	930			1035	dk antique blue
∩	932	∩		1033	antique blue
4	947	4		330	orange
▲	986			246	vy dk green
7	987	7		244	dk green
H	988	H		243	green
O	989			242	lt green
+	996	+		433	electric blue
/	3753	/		1031	baby blue
✳	3801			1098	salmon
2	3820	2		306	gold
★	3821	★		305	lt gold

▨ Grey area indicates last row of previous section of design.

Family Fun was stitched on a 12" x 18" piece of 14 count White Aida (design size 9" x 15"). Three strands of floss were used for Cross Stitch and one strand for Backstitch. The design was personalized using the alphabet on page 31 and two strands of DMC 310 floss and made into a stocking.

Stocking Finishing Instructions
Using your stitched stocking as a guide, trace the stocking shape onto tracing paper for a pattern. Add ¹/₂" seam allowance to the pattern and cut out. Use the pattern to cut one backing piece and two lining pieces from fabric. Position and pin the pattern to the wrong side of the stitched piece. Use a fabric marking pen to draw around the pattern. Remove the pattern and cut on the drawn line.

Matching raw edges, baste ¹/₄" dia. purchased cording with attached seam allowance to the right side of the stocking front.

Matching right sides and leaving the top edge open, use a ¹/₂" seam allowance to sew the stitched piece and backing fabric together. Clip the seam allowances at curves and turn the stocking right side out. Press the top edge of the stocking ¹/₂" to the wrong side.

Instructions continued on page 13.

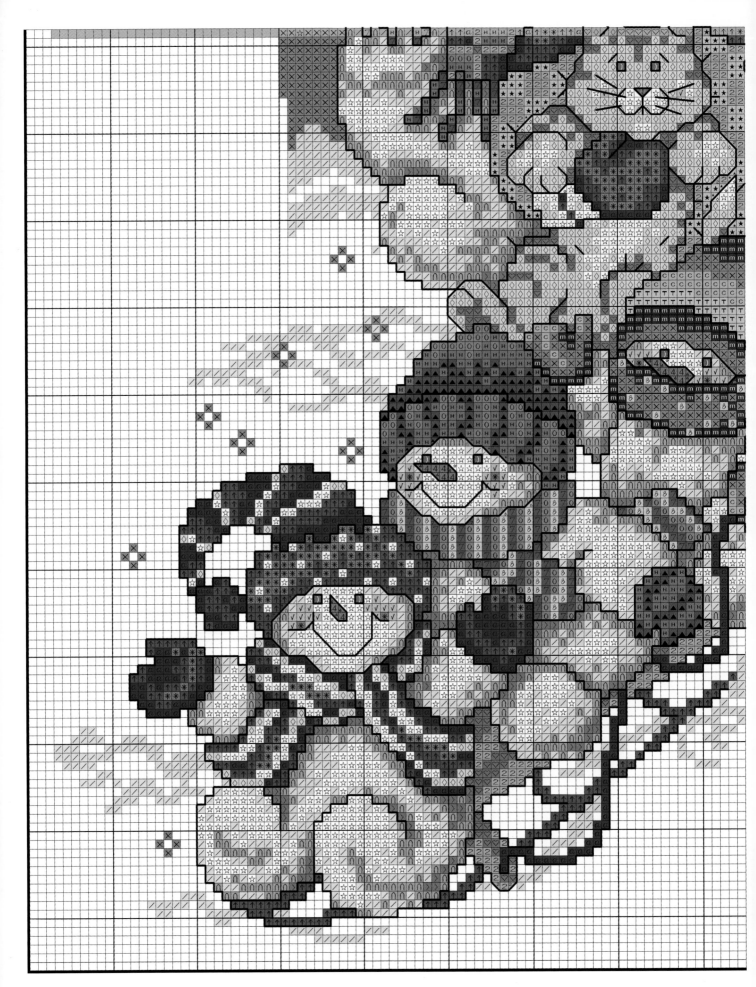

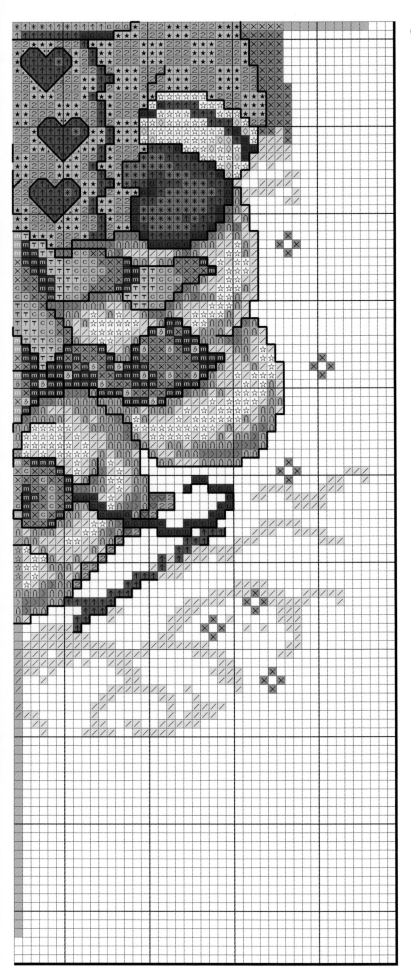

Family Fun

X DMC	¼X	B'ST	ANC.	COLOR
☆ blanc	☆		2	white
☽ 310	◪	╱	403	black
↑ 321	◪		9046	red
√ 353	√		6	pink
◇ 677	◇		886	tan
♡ 680	◪		901	dk gold
8 726	8		295	yellow
m 796	m		133	dk blue
✕ 798	✕		131	blue
T 800			144	vy lt blue
C 809			130	lt blue
a 816	◪		1005	maroon
⟩ 930	◪		1035	dk antique blue
∩ 932	∩		1033	antique blue
4 947	4		330	orange
▲ 986	◪		246	vy dk green
7 987	◪		244	dk green
H 988	H		243	green
O 989			242	lt green
✛ 996	◪		433	electric blue
╱ 3753	╱		1031	baby blue
✳ 3801			1098	salmon
2 3820	2		306	gold
★ 3821	★		305	lt gold

▨ Grey area indicates last row of previous section of design.

Finishing Instructions continued from page 11.
Matching raw edges, baste ¹/4" dia. purchased cording with attached seam allowance to the right side of the stocking top. Matching right sides and leaving the top edge open, use a ⁵/8" seam allowance to sew lining pieces together. Trim the seam allowances close to stitching. Do not turn the lining right side out. Press the top edge of the lining ¹/2" to the wrong side.

For a hanger, cut a 2" x 6" piece of fabric. Press each long edge of the fabric strip ¹/2" to the center. Matching long edges, fold the hanger in half and sew close to the folded edges. Matching short edges, fold the hanger in half and whipstitch to the inside of the stocking at the right seam.

With wrong sides together, place lining inside stocking. Blind stitch lining to stocking.

Stitch Count (123w x 210h)

14 count	9"	x	15"
16 count	7³/4"	x	13¹/4"
18 count	7"	x	11³/4"

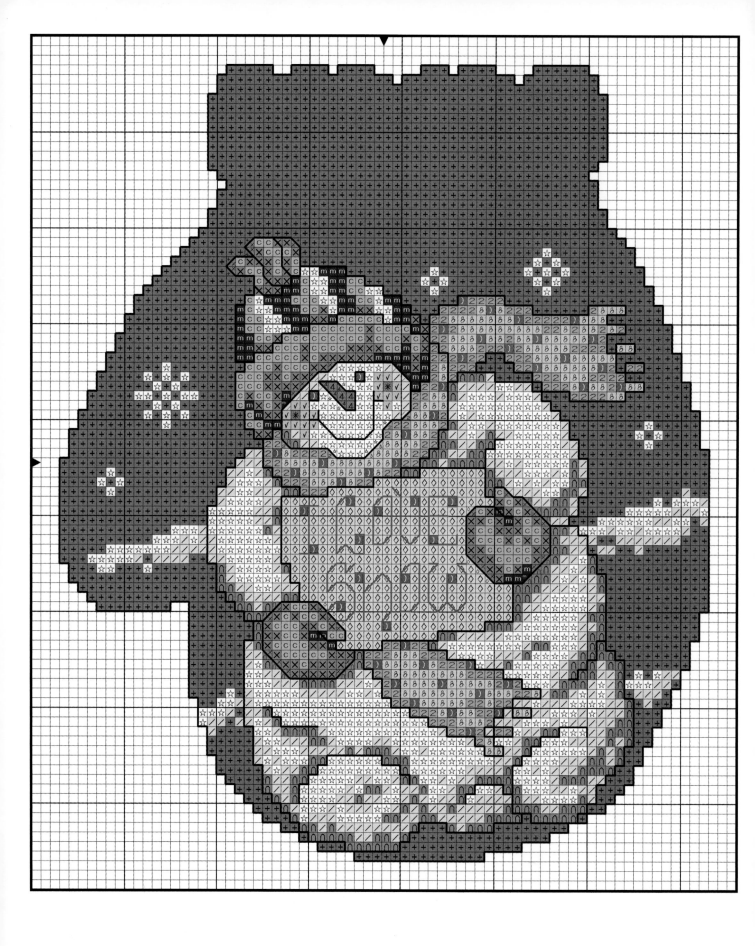

X	DMC	1/4X	B'ST	ANC.	COLOR
☆	blanc	☆		2	white
)	310		/	403	black
	310		/*	403	black
√	353			6	pink
◇	677	◇		886	tan
8	726	8		295	yellow
m	796	m		133	dk blue
×	798	×		131	blue
C	809			130	lt blue
∩	932	∩		1033	antique blue
4	947	4		330	orange
+	996	4		433	electric blue
/	3753	/		1031	baby blue
✳	3801			1098	salmon
2	3820	2		306	gold

* Use 2 strands of floss.

I Love Snow was stitched on an 8" x 9" piece of 14 count White Aida (design size 5" x 6"). Three strands of floss were used for Cross Stitch and one strand for Backstitch except where noted in the key. I Love Snow was made into an ornament.

Ornament Finishing Instructions

Trim stitched piece to the desired finished size plus $1/2$" on all sides. Cut fabric for backing the same size. Matching right sides and raw edges and using a $1/2$" seam allowance, sew stitched piece to backing fabric leaving an opening for turning. Clip seam allowances. Turn right side out, and press. Stuff ornament with polyester fiberfill. Slipstitch opening closed.

Stitch Count (70w x 83h)

14 count	5"	x	6"
16 count	$4^1/2$"	x	$5^1/4$"
18 count	4"	x	$4^3/4$"

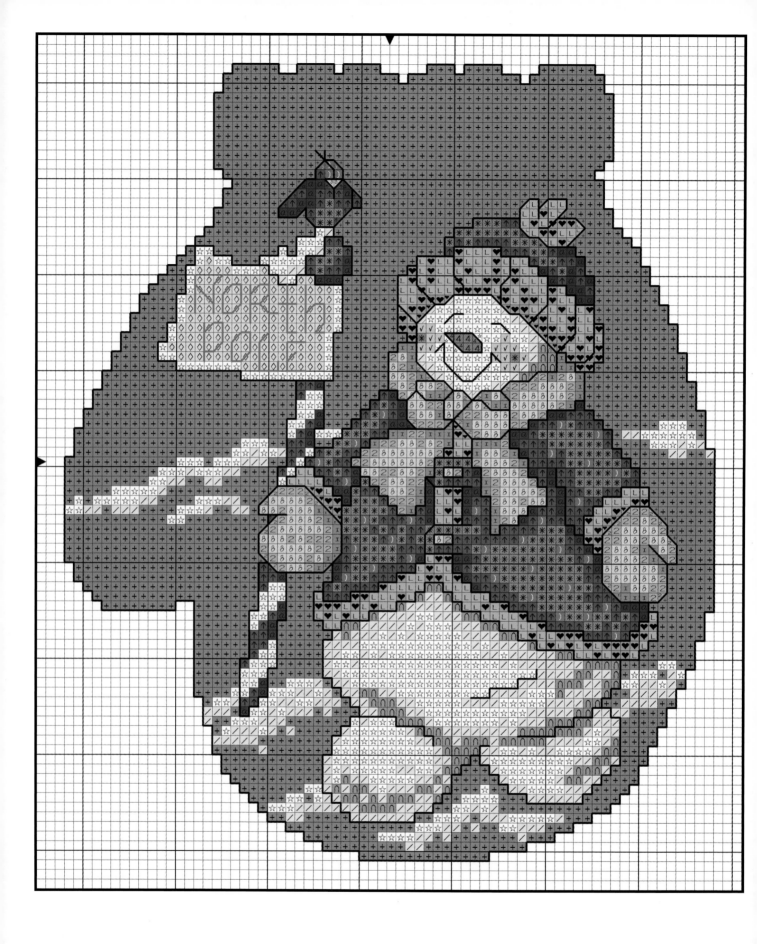

North Pole

X	DMC	¼X	B'ST	ANC.	COLOR
☆	blanc			2	white
L	164				lt green
)	310		/	403	black
	310		/*	403	black
↑	321			9046	red
√	353			6	pink
◇	677			886	tan
♥	703			238	green
8	726			295	yellow
a	816			1005	maroon
n	932			1033	antique blue
4	947			330	orange
+	996			433	electric blue
/	3753			1031	baby blue
✱	3801			1098	salmon
2	3820			306	gold
I	3852			306	dk gold

*Use 2 strands of floss.

North Pole was stitched on an 8" x 9" piece of 14 count White Aida (design size 5" x 6"). Three strands of floss were used for Cross Stitch and one strand for Backstitch except where noted in the key. North Pole was made into an ornament.

Ornament Finishing Instructions
Trim the stitched piece to desired finished size plus ¹/₂" on all sides. Cut fabric for backing the same size. Matching right sides and raw edges and using a ¹/₂" seam allowance, sew the stitched piece to backing fabric, leaving an opening for turning. Clip seam allowances. Turn right side out and press. Stuff the ornament with polyester fiberfill and slipstitch the opening closed.

Stitch Count (70w x 83h)

14 count	5"	x	6"
16 count	4¹/₂"	x	5¹/₄"
18 count	4"	x	4³/₄"

18

Shoveling Snow

X	DMC	¼X	B'ST	ANC.	COLOR
☆	blanc			2	white
☽	310		✓	403	black
↑	321			9046	red
√	353			6	pink
3	415			398	grey
♥	680			901	dk gold
8	726			295	yellow
a	816			1005	maroon
⋂	932			1033	antique blue
7	987			244	dk green
H	988			243	green
0	989			242	lt green
+	996			433	electric blue
╱	3753			1031	baby blue
✳	3801			1098	salmon
2	3820			306	gold

Shoveling Snow was stitched on an 8" x 9" piece of 14 count White Aida (design size 5" x 6"). Three strands of floss were used for Cross Stitch and one strand for Backstitch. Shoveling Snow was made into an ornament.

Ornament Finishing Instructions
Trim the stitched piece to desired finished size plus 1/2" on all sides. Cut fabric for backing the same size. Matching right sides and raw edges and using a 1/2" seam allowance, sew the stitched piece to backing fabric, leaving an opening for turning. Clip seam allowances. Turn right side out and press. Stuff the ornament with polyester fiberfill and slipstitch the opening closed.

Stitch Count (70w x 83h)

14 count	5"	x 6"
16 count	4 1/2"	x 5 1/4"
18 count	4"	x 4 3/4"

Jingle Bells

X	DMC	1/4X	B'ST	ANC.	COLOR
☆	blanc			2	white
L	164				vy lt green
)	310		/	403	black
⊥	317			400	grey
↑	321			9046	red
√	353			6	pink
3	415			398	lt grey
↔	676			891	antique gold
♡	680			901	dk antique gold
8	726			295	yellow
m	796			133	vy dk blue
X	798			131	dk blue
T	800			144	lt blue
C	809			130	blue
a	816			1005	maroon
∩	932			1033	antique blue
4	947			330	orange
▲	986			246	vy dk green
7	987			244	dk green
H	988			243	green
O	989			242	lt green
+	996			433	electric blue
/	3753			1031	baby blue
✳	3801			1098	salmon
2	3820			306	gold
<	3822			295	lt gold
I	3852			306	dk gold

Grey area indicates last row of previous section of design.

Jingle Bells was stitched on a 25" x 9¹/₂" piece of 14 count White Aida (design size 22" x 6¹/₂"). Three strands of floss were used for Cross Stitch and one strand for Backstitch. The design was custom framed.

Stitch Count (306w x 91h)

14 count	22" x 6¹/₂"
16 count	19¹/₄" x 5³/₄"
18 count	17" x 5¹/₄"

Chart continued on pgs. 24-26.

Diagram

Section 1	Section 2	Section 3	Section 4	Section 5